Especially for

_____

From

_____

Date

_____

# Encouragement for a Mother's Heart

## Soul Refreshment for Moms

BARBOUR
PUBLISHING

Devotional selections from *365 Daily Whispers of Wisdom for Mothers of Preschoolers*, published by Barbour Publishing, Inc.

Prayers by Rachel Quillin are from *Power Prayers for Mothers*, published by Barbour Publishing, Inc. Prayers by Donna K. Maltese are from *Power Prayers to Start Your Day*, published by Barbour Publishing, Inc. Prayers by Jackie M. Johnson are from *Power Prayers for Women*, published by Barbour Publishing, Inc.

Scripture quotations marked KJV are taken from the King James Version of the Bible.

Scripture quotations marked MSG are from *THE MESSAGE*. Copyright © by Eugene H. Peterson 1993, 1994, 1995, 1996, 2000, 2001, 2002. Used by permission of NavPress Publishing Group.

Scripture quotations marked NASB are taken from the New American Standard Bible, © 1960, 1962, 1963, 1968, 1971, 1972, 1973, 1975, 1977, 1995 by The Lockman Foundation. Used by permission.

Scripture quotations marked NIV are taken from the HOLY BIBLE, NEW INTERNATIONAL VERSION®. NIV®. Copyright © 1973, 1978, 1984 by International Bible Society. Used by permission of Zondervan. All rights reserved.

Scripture quotations marked NLT are taken from the *Holy Bible*, New Living Translation, copyright © 1996, 2004. Used by permission of Tyndale House Publishers, Inc. Wheaton, Illinois 60189, U.S.A. All rights reserved.

Scripture quotations marked NRSV are taken from the New Revised Standard Version Bible, copyright 1989, Division of Christian Education of the National Council of the Churches of Christ in the United States of America. Used by permission. All rights reserved.

Scripture quotations marked TLB are taken from The Living Bible © 1971. Used by permission of Tyndale House Publishers, Inc. Wheaton, Illinois 60189. All rights reserved.

Published by Barbour Publishing, Inc., P.O. Box 719, Uhrichsville, Ohio 44683, www.barbourbooks.com

*Our mission is to publish and distribute inspirational products offering exceptional value and biblical encouragement to the masses.*

Member of the
Evangelical Christian
Publishers Association

Printed in the United States.

# Contents

God loves you desperately.
Live like you believe it.

UNKNOWN

# Faith Is . .

Faith is not wishful thinking, grasping at straws, or our last resort. Faith is being sure and certain. Faith is taking God at His word. It is knowing that God will bring to pass that which He promises. By faith Noah built an ark, even though it had not yet rained. By faith Abraham left his homeland and ventured to a foreign country, even though he could not see it. By faith Moses led the people out of Egypt, even though he felt unqualified as a leader. These men of faith did not know what the future would hold, yet they knew the One who holds the future.

Faith requires a leap, a jump. Everything is not neatly figured out. If we had all the answers, faith wouldn't be required.

In response to what the Lord is asking us to do or believe, in faith we simply say yes. Like Peter, we decide to step out of the boat as we keep our eyes on Him. We trust God, knowing that He will keep His promises.

When we step out in faith, we are given a glimpse of the spiritual realm. We "see" the invisible. We can be sure and certain because our trust is placed in the Lord. He will remain faithful. We can stake our lives on His trustworthiness. Let's step out and believe Him. Let's exercise faith.

*Julie Rayburn*

*Now faith is being sure of what we hope for
and certain of what we do not see.*

HEBREWS 11:1 NIV

# Believing

## Be Encouraged, Mom!

Take a much deserved
time-out for yourself. . .
You spend so much of your
time doing for others, Mom.
Now it's your turn to indulge a
little and refresh your spirit.

# With All Your Heart

Lord, from the time my children were babies,
I've committed them to Your care. When they
were quite small, they looked to me for all the
answers. As they grow, they realize that I don't
know everything. I want them to understand,
however, that You do and that everything is in
Your control. Help them to commit daily to
trusting You and to recognize that they don't
have to face life alone.

*Rachel Quillin*

*"Look! I have been standing at the door
and I am constantly knocking.
If anyone hears me calling him and opens the door,
I will come in and fellowship with him and he with me."*

REVELATION 3:20 TLB

# Open the Door

Jesus is knocking on the door of our hearts. He will not barge in uninvited. What is our response? Do we eagerly invite Him in? Or would we prefer that He leave us alone? If we yearn for His help, we beckon Him to enter. If we desire to know Him more, we hasten Him in. But if we think we can handle life on our own, we ignore the knocking. Or perhaps we feel unworthy to receive such a noble visitor.

Whether we care to admit it or not, we desperately need God's daily presence. His guidance, wisdom, and counsel are invaluable because He is omniscient. When we open our heart's door and invite Him in, He walks with us throughout the day. Guidance is given. Peace is imparted. Strength is obtained.

You may feel that you are handling life just fine without His help. Are you really? You may feel unworthy of His presence. Yet you are His valuable creation! God loves you so much He gave His life so that you can enter into a personal relationship with Him. He's standing at the door and knocking. Why not invite Him in?

*Julie Rayburn*

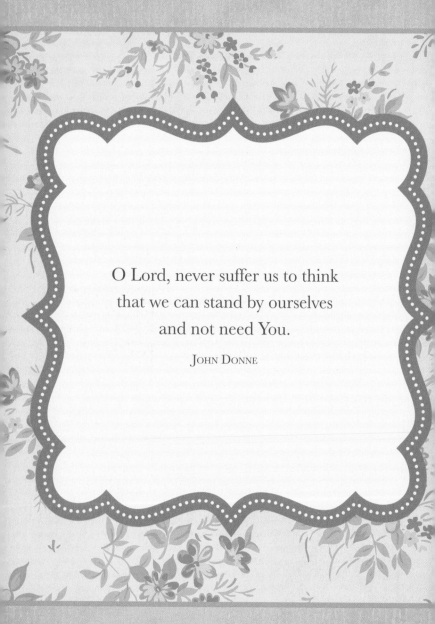

O Lord, never suffer us to think
that we can stand by ourselves
and not need You.

JOHN DONNE

# A Reason to Believe

You are the best example of faith I could hope for, Lord Jesus. You knew all that You would face, and You went through with it anyway. All that You've ever done or will do gives me a reason to trust You. I can recall many times that one day I'll receive the ultimate reward—eternity with You.

*Rachel Quillin*

*Trust in the LORD with all thine heart;*
*and lean not unto thine own understanding.*

PROVERBS 3:5 KJV

Blessings

*Then Peter and the other apostles answered and said,*
*we ought to obey God rather than men.*

ACTS 5:29 KJV

# Café Mom

"Come on in! Coffee is brewing, and a delectably sweet bit of something gooey is coming out of the oven. At Café Mom, you'll find rest, peace, comfort, and the answers you need to solve all of life's problems."

Moms often feel as if the image of "Café Mom" is what a "good mom" is expected to project. They look around their homes strewn with toys and at the piles of laundry yet to be folded and the dishes still to be washed. They fervently hope that no one pops in for a quick visit. They want to hang the CLOSED sign on the door to Café Mom because they just can't serve up those tall orders for yet another day.

But the expectations of other people are not how God determines value. He rates time with our kids, moments of prayer, and times of reading scripture as far more valuable than finished laundry and a pristine kitchen sink.

Café Mom is a wonderful ideal, and surely it is even a reality sometimes. But Jesus wants us to place His values above the expectations of others. Honor attained from pleasing people is fleeting and empty. His way is much easier, for it is the way to a peaceful heart and a life rich in the blessings of Christ.

*Nicole O'Dell*

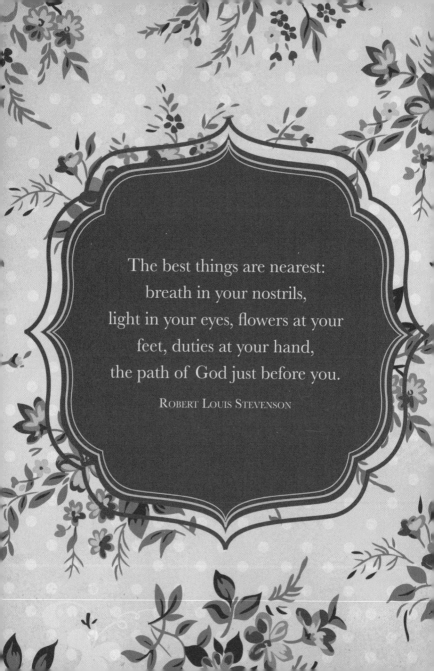

The best things are nearest:
breath in your nostrils,
light in your eyes, flowers at your
feet, duties at your hand,
the path of God just before you.

ROBERT LOUIS STEVENSON

## Choosing Life

Lord, this day I choose life—I choose to live
and work and have my being in You. Instead of
looking at all that I don't have, I choose to look
at all that You have blessed me with—family,
friends, a home, a job, clothes on my back, food
in my belly. . . . Oh Lord, the list is endless.
Thank You so much for being my life today
and every day! I cling to You each and every
moment. Live through me!

*Donna K. Maltese*

"Don't store up treasures here on earth
where they can erode away or may be stolen.
Store them in heaven
where they will never lose their value,
and are safe from thieves."

Matthew 6:19–20 tlb

# Stuff

The bumper sticker on the red Porsche read: THE ONE WHO DIES WITH THE MOST TOYS WINS. Our culture is obsessed with the accumulation of "stuff." Second homes are commonplace. Clothes are bulging from dresser drawers. Storage facilities on every street corner are overflowing with unusable earthly treasures.

Jesus reminds us that everything we see is temporary. None of our earthly possessions will enter heaven's gates. Everything will be left behind. Then why do we spend so much time, money, and energy obtaining temporary treasures? Jesus encourages us to concentrate on eternal treasures instead. Spending time studying God's Word and growing closer to Him is a wise investment. Pouring our lives into people will allow us to reap lasting benefits. Using material blessings to spiritually impact others is commended by God.

Rather than storing up "stuff," let's pass it on so that others may be blessed. Clean out a closet. Empty a drawer. Give to those less fortunate. Then focus on things that will last forever and never lose their value. When we store up heavenly treasures, we will be blessed in this life and in the life to come.

*Julie Rayburn*

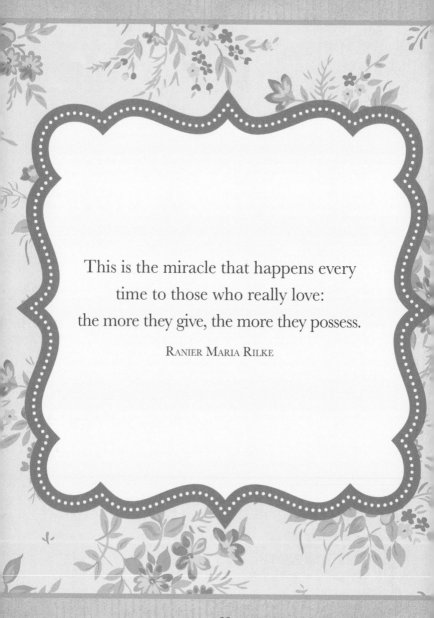

This is the miracle that happens every
time to those who really love:
the more they give, the more they possess.

RANIER MARIA RILKE

## Sharing My Blessings

Lord, You have blessed me and the works of my
hands. I am very grateful to You for all that I have.
As You bless me, I am able to bless others in whatever
way I can. What a feeling to know that I am able
to help expand Your kingdom! Help me to tithe my
talents, monies, and time, all to Your glory. For Thine
is the kingdom and the power, forever and ever.

*Donna K. Maltese*

*"Every man shall give as he is able,*
*according to the blessing of the LORD your God*
*which He has given you."*

DEUTERONOMY 16:17 NASB

# Comfort
# &
# Contentment

*Therefore my heart is glad,*
*and my glory rejoiceth:*
*my flesh also shall rest in hope.*

PSALM 16:9 KJV

# Refreshment

Do you ever feel like you're being pulled in a dozen different ways? Before your eyes open in the morning, one of the children is crying or calling for you. Someone in your family asks you a favor. The church wants you to help with a program. A friend needs someone to talk to. At the end of the day, the kids need help getting ready for bed, and your husband wants you to spend time with him.

When you finally crawl into bed, you are exhausted. In the midst of caring for little ones and doing what you can for others, you've had no time for God. Guilt rears up, because you know that spending time with God is the most important part of every day.

God never makes demands on us. He invites us to come to Him. He is always there waiting for us. God understands the necessities of our daily lives. He knows the needs of our children, families, and friends.

When we fall into bed at the end of the day, we have the opportunity to take a few moments of spiritual refreshment with God before getting much needed physical sleep. We can relax in His care, knowing there will come a day when we'll have more time with Him.

*Nancy Farrier*

The Well of Providence is deep.
It's the buckets we bring to
it that are small.

MARY WEBB

# Finding Contentment

Lord, please help me to find my contentment in You. I don't want to be defined by "stuff"—the things I own or what I do. May my greatest happiness in life be knowing who You are and who I am in Christ. May I treasure the simple things in life, those things that bring me peace. With Your grace, I rest secure. You, Lord, are my satisfaction.

*Jackie M. Johnson*

And He said to His disciples,
"For this reason I say to you,
do not worry about your life,
as to what you will eat;
nor for your body,
as to what you will put on."

LUKE 12:22 NASB

# Anxiety-free Contentment

According to Proverbs 31, mothers are to feed and clothe their families.

In Bible times these tasks took a woman's time and energy, especially when she had to plant the garden, haggle with vendors at the market, and make clothes by hand. Without the benefit of modern conveniences to deliver and preserve food, and given the threat of famine and pestilence, feeding a family could cause a mother much anxiety.

Imagine the reaction of the women of Palestine when Jesus said, "Don't worry about what you're going to eat and wear. God will give you these needs as you seek Him." What relief they must have felt!

Have we forgotten this simple truth? Even though we feed and clothe our families with relative ease compared to our foremothers, do we still get stressed because our children wear hand-me-downs or eat leftovers twice in one week?

God promises to meet our basic needs. If our families need more than hand-me-downs and leftovers, God will provide them. Tap into the joy of this guarantee.

Be content with what you have, and believe God. If you really *need* more, He'll give it.

*Helen Widger Middlebrooke*

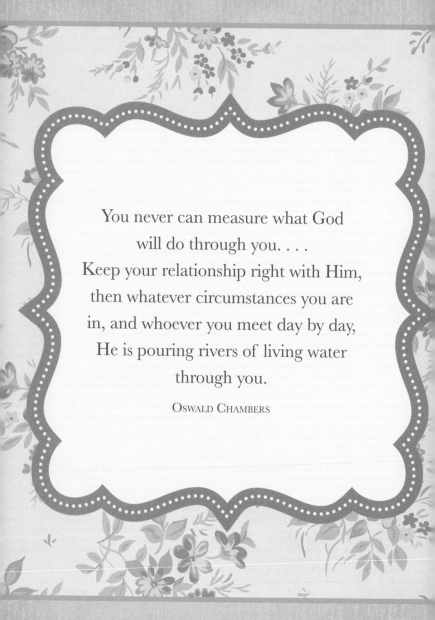

You never can measure what God
will do through you. . . .
Keep your relationship right with Him,
then whatever circumstances you are
in, and whoever you meet day by day,
He is pouring rivers of living water
through you.

OSWALD CHAMBERS

## Lifting Manna

Here I am once more, Lord, asking You again this morning to meet my needs. I've been so down, Lord, with all the things that have been happening in the world, in my home, in my family. Help me again today to go forth, to gather as much as I need and be content with that. Hear my prayer, O Lord, and help me day by day.

*Donna K. Maltese*

*"God has been very gracious to me.*
*I have more than enough."*

GENESIS 33:11 NLT

Love

*"For God so loved the world that he gave his one and only Son, that whoever believes in him shall not perish but have eternal life."*

JOHN 3:16 NIV

# Jesus Loves Me

"Jesus loves me, this I know, for the Bible tells me so. Little ones to Him belong. They are weak, but He is strong."

We've probably sung that song dozens of times with our little ones, but have we considered its message? It actually teaches four huge doctrinal truths. First, we see that Jesus loves us. He loves us so much that He gave His own life as a sacrifice (1 John 3:16). Next, the song assures us that the Bible is worthy of being believed, for its words are true. We can be confident of this, because scripture is God-breathed (2 Timothy 3:16).

Third, this song reminds us that even the little children belong to Him. The Bible tells us that our faith is to be like that of a child, and we are to come to Him as little children (Mark 10:15).

Finally, we are reminded of one of the greatest promises of hope for the believer, that His strength is made perfect when we are weakest. We could not live an effective Christian life in our own strength (2 Corinthians 12:9).

Allow your faith to become like that of a child, and seek Him in the simple things. Let even the words of a simple children's song bathe your soul in comforting truth.

*Nicole O'Dell*

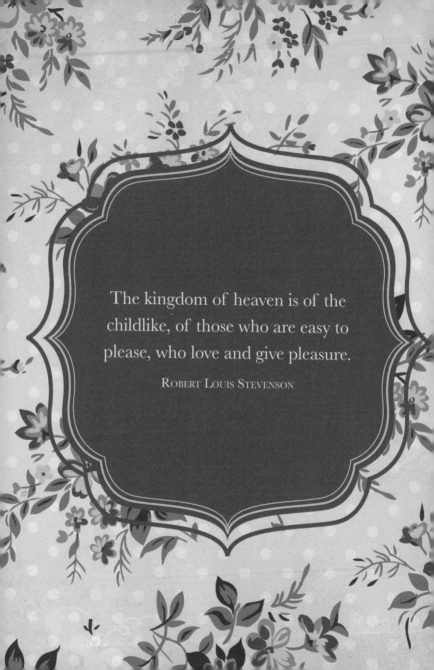

The kingdom of heaven is of the childlike, of those who are easy to please, who love and give pleasure.

ROBERT LOUIS STEVENSON

# With All My Life

Jehovah God, You are the creator of all. Your power cannot be exceeded. You are above all, yet You want a personal love relationship with me. This truth is hard to comprehend, yet You require my total, undivided love. You want my entire devotion—my heart, soul, and strength. I cannot deny them. You, who have given me both physical and spiritual life, deserve only my best.

*Rachel Quillin*

*I will greatly rejoice in the L*ORD*, my soul shall be joyful in my God; for he hath clothed me with the garments of salvation, he hath covered me with the robe of righteousness.*

ISAIAH 61:10 KJV

# Treasured Moments

Have you ever watched your child and been struck by the depth of love you have for him? This is a love so intense it is almost a physical ache. At that moment you may want nothing other than to spend more time with your toddler, watching him and getting to know him as he grows.

Each developmental age of a child is different, full of surprises, trials, and delights. We can stand in wonder as we watch our offspring learn new skills or discover the world around them. We thrill over first hugs or kisses, never getting enough and thankful for each one bestowed. Even the independent "do-it-myself" stages can charm us as our child grows.

When we stop to contemplate the gifts God has given us—salvation, love, grace, mercy, and more—we are filled with wonder. The God who created everything loves us enough to want to have a personal, intimate relationship with us. We can rejoice, knowing that God will always delight in us as much as we delight in Him. He, too, is thankful for each expression of love we extend to Him.

*Nancy Farrier*

Your only treasures are those
which you carry in your heart.

DEMOPHILUS

## Obedience and Blessing

Oh wise God, all that You've commanded is for
a purpose. You know what is best for me and for
everyone else. You've promised that if I obey You,
my children will be blessed. I could not give them a
greater gift! Today, because I love You and because I
want Your best for my children, I rededicate myself to
living according to Your Word.

*Rachel Quillin*

*Above all, love each other deeply,*
*because love covers over a multitude of sins.*

1 PETER 4:8 NIV

Peace

*"Peace I leave with you; my peace I give you.
I do not give to you as the world gives.
Do not let your hearts be troubled and
do not be afraid."*

JOHN 14:27 NIV

# A Peaceful Life

What gives you peace? A conflict-free life? No stress or worries? Obedient children?

We know that in this life there will be conflict, stress, worries, and disobedient children. There is no way we can avoid the sinful nature of this world. However, in the challenges of raising children, Jesus has left us with and desires to continually give us peace. The stipulation is that the type of peace the world gives—the temporal, brief, counterfeit peace—is not God's eternal peace. When we believe in our hearts and confess with our lips that Jesus is Lord, we are saved (Romans 10:9–10). We automatically are in a peaceful relationship with the Lord. As believers we have Jesus' Spirit (John 15:5), the Holy Spirit (John 14:26), the Prince of Peace (Isaiah 9:6), indwelling us. With the eternal security of being at peace with the Lord and peace indwelling us, we are then free to "not worry about anything, but in everything by prayer and supplication with thanksgiving let [our] requests be made known to God. And the peace of God, which surpasses all understanding, will guard [our] hearts and [our] minds in Christ Jesus" (Philippians 4:6–7 NRSV).

*Tina Elacqua*

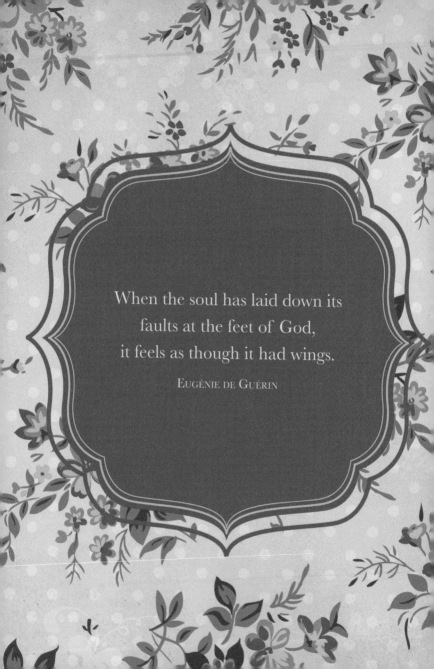

When the soul has laid down its
faults at the feet of God,
it feels as though it had wings.

EUGÉNIE DE GUÉRIN

# Live in Peace

We have a houseful of people with different personalities, ideas, and attitudes, dear God. Sometimes that can be a lot of fun, but it can also be confusing. Still, You've commanded us to live in peace, and of course, that's what we want, too. Please give us the ability to work together. Show us when we should compromise. Fill our home with love and peace.

*Rachel Quillin*

*"In My Father's house are many dwelling places;*
*if it were not so, I would have told you;*
*for I go to prepare a place for you."*

JOHN 14:2 NASB

# Your Special Dwelling Place

Moms spend much of their time maintaining their homes: cooking, cleaning, laundering, organizing—the list is endless. Because sin entered into the world, work came along as a consequence. Even now you're probably multitasking—perhaps deciding what to make for dinner while you try to catch up on your time with God.

But take a moment to rest in the promise Jesus gave in John 14:2. He informs us that there is a place waiting for us that will require nothing on our part. Jesus tells us that in His Father's house, there are plenty of rooms for everyone—no one has to fight over who gets the top bunk—and there will be a place tailor-made for you. Just imagine Him talking with God and saying, "Father, [insert your own name here] will be joining us soon. I'd like to make a special room just for her."

What a joy to know that Jesus has found time to prepare a place for *you*—one that you will never have to worry about painting, decorating, or cleaning!

*Jennifer Hahn*

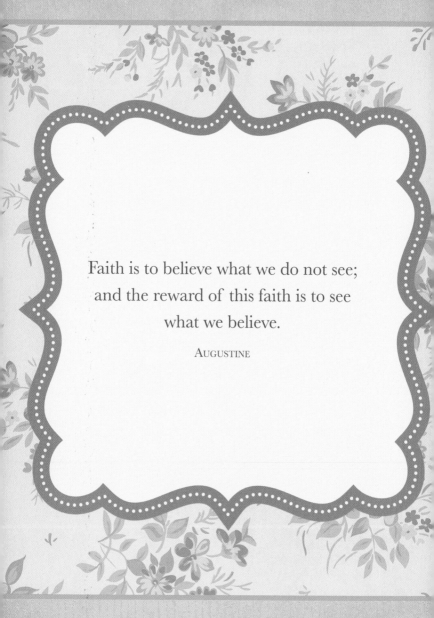

Faith is to believe what we do not see;
and the reward of this faith is to see
what we believe.

AUGUSTINE

## The Peace That Brings Life

Lord, I thank You for the peace that restores me
mentally, emotionally, and physically. Your peace brings
wholeness. When my heart is restless, my health suffers.
But when I am at peace, You restore my entire body. I
can breathe easier, I can relax, and I can smile again
because I know everything's going to be all right. You
are in control. I thank You that Your peace brings life.

*Jackie M. Johnson*

*"The LORD bless you and keep you; the LORD make his face shine upon you and be gracious to you; the LORD turn his face toward you and give you peace."*

NUMBERS 6:24–26 NIV

Prayer

*"If ye then, being evil, know how to give good gifts unto your children, how much more shall your Father which is in heaven give good things to them that ask him?"*

MATTHEW 7:11 KJV

# How Much More?

When we pray, what do we expect?

Do we truly believe that God hears and answers prayers, or do we think He has a heavenly voice mail system that He ignores?

That latter idea may seem preposterous to a child of God. Yet how often do we approach prayer, thinking that God won't answer, or worse, thinking that He may send us an answer that will be hard for us to accept?

We have not, James says, because we ask not (James 4:2). And sometimes we don't get what we ask because we ask with wrong motives (verse 3). Or we ask in unbelief (1:6–8), not knowing the heart of God.

God loves us in the same way and perhaps more than we love our children. As we would never give our children anything bad, God will never—*ever*—give us anything bad. As James 1:17 says, "Every *good* gift and every perfect gift is from above, and cometh down from the Father of lights" (KJV, emphasis added).

So ask. Believe. And receive so much more.

*Helen Widger Middlebrooke*

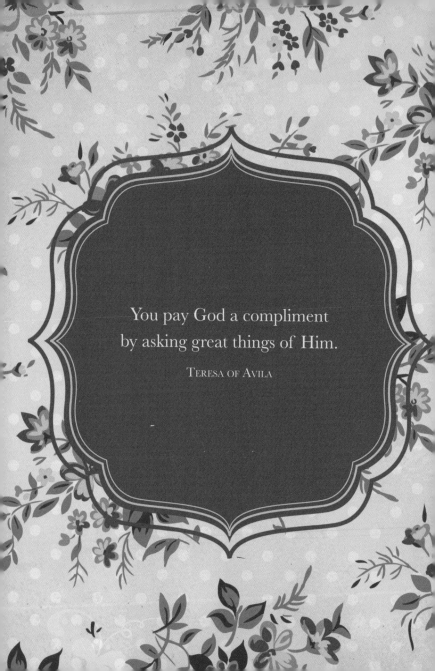

You pay God a compliment
by asking great things of Him.

TERESA OF AVILA

## Making Prayer a Priority

Lord, I feel like a withered plant with dry, brown leaves. Help me connect with You in prayer so I can grow strong and healthy—inside and out— like a vibrant green tree. You are my source of living water. Teach me to be still, to listen, to absorb what You want to reveal to me in this time of inward filling. In this holy conversation, may I find freedom, peace, and joy—and a closer walk with You.

*Jackie M. Johnson*

Then Eli discerned that the LORD was calling the boy.
And Eli said to Samuel, "Go lie down, and it shall be if
He calls you, that you shall say, 'Speak, LORD, for Your
servant is listening.'" So Samuel went and lay down in
his place. Then the LORD came and stood and called as
at other times, "Samuel! Samuel!" And Samuel said,
"Speak, for Your servant is listening."

1 SAMUEL 3:8–10 NASB

# Yes, Lord, I'm Listening

Samuel was just a boy when he woke up hearing someone call his name. Three times he woke Eli up, assuming it was Eli who called him, and was promptly sent back to bed! After the third time, Eli realized that it was God who was calling Samuel's name. Wisely, he redirected Samuel to listen to God.

As we are teaching our children to pray, are we teaching them to listen? To recognize God's voice—the small stirrings in our hearts that guide us to God's greater path?

God had a plan for Samuel's life. He promises the same for our children, calling each one by name. As we encourage our children to listen for God's quiet voice, we make it easier for them to hear His call over the shouts of the world.

May we all strive to be like Eli, who encouraged Samuel to say yes to God's calling.

*Suzanne Woods Fisher*

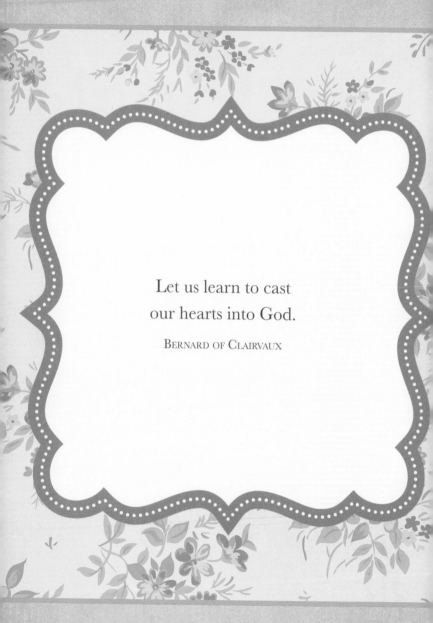

Let us learn to cast
our hearts into God.

BERNARD OF CLAIRVAUX

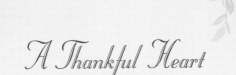

# A Thankful Heart

Lord, You are my God—and it is my joy to give You
my inner heart. Cleanse me, fill me, heal me, and help
me to live with a joyful, thankful heart. I want to be a
woman of prayer. I want to make a difference in my
world. For all You are and all You do, I am grateful.
I give You praise for the blessings in my life.

*Jackie M. Johnson*

*Be joyful always; pray continually;*
*give thanks in all circumstances,*
*for this is God's will for you in Christ Jesus.*

1 Thessalonians 5:16–18 NIV

Protection

*For in the day of trouble he will keep me safe in his dwelling; he will hide me in the shelter of his tabernacle and set me high upon a rock.*

PSALM 27:5 NIV

# Safe in Christ

*Crack! Boom!* "Mommy, I'm scared!" the little girl cried as the thunder clapped outside her bedroom window. Her mother calmly replied, "Honey, the thunder and lightning are out there. We are safe in here." Knowing that an explanation of the physics of static electricity would not alleviate her daughter's fears, the mother simply provided a safe haven from the storm.

The storms of life have a way of frightening us also. Perhaps an upcoming surgery or financial difficulties are looming overhead. Maybe marital stress or child-rearing issues have cast a dark cloud over our homes. We may not understand what is happening. It's dark. It's chaotic. It's ominous. In His wisdom, the Lord tells us all we need to know: We are safe because He is with us.

Seek shelter from the storm. Run to the Lord's dwelling. He will keep you safe and grant you peace. He will calm your heart, reassuring you of His protection. Like thunder and lightning, the storms we face in life are temporary. The Lord remains. Therefore, we are eternally safe in His dwelling. Come in out of the storm.

*Julie Rayburn*

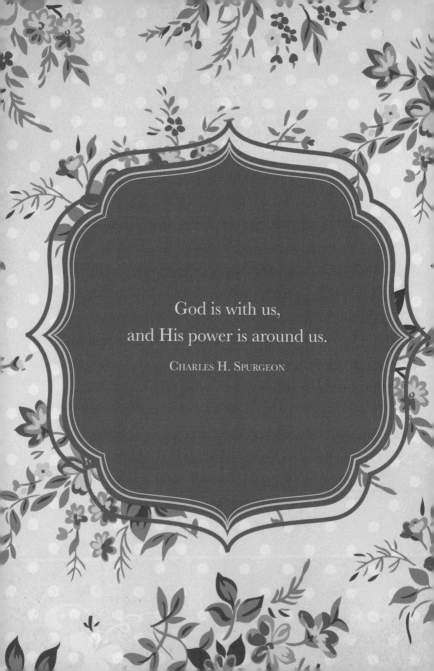

God is with us,
and His power is around us.

CHARLES H. SPURGEON

# Protection from Evil

It is well with my soul, for I am Your child and You protect me from all evils. I come to You, pouring out my heart, sharing my fears and worries. Take these fears from me and shepherd me to a place close beside You. Snuggle up close to me and fill me with the comfort of Your Word. Help me to be still and listen to Your advice. I want to know what You want me to do. Dispel the negative thoughts and fill me with Your Word, for that is the power that will get me through this day and the days to come.

*Donna K. Maltese*

*The angel of the LORD appeared to [Gideon] and said to him, "The LORD is with you, O valiant warrior."*

JUDGES 6:12 NASB

# Show Me a Sign!

Gideon's appearance on the biblical scene seemed almost comical. The angel of the Lord sought Gideon out, bestowing on him the title "valiant warrior." Gideon was anything *but* a valiant warrior! Immediately, Gideon started objecting. He doubted that the Lord was really with him. He questioned the battle plan that the angel of the Lord spelled out to him. He pointed out that his family was from a very weak tribe. "My clan is the weakest. . .and I am the least in my family" (Judges 6:15 NIV). As if God didn't know!

After three or four objections, it would seem reasonable for the angel of the Lord to move on to a more willing warrior. But no! Patiently, oh so patiently, He dispelled Gideon's concerns. The Lord answered, "I will be with you" (verse 16 NIV).

God was not put off by Gideon's feelings of inadequacy or shallow faith. He would provide what Gideon needed when he needed it. Even courage! In fact, He encouraged Gideon to "Go in the strength you have" (verse 14 NIV).

Rare is the mother who isn't overwhelmed at times by the task of raising children. This is a long, hard job. But God never intended us to go it alone. He is with us, patiently encouraging us, providing the strength and wisdom we need just as we need it.

*Suzanne Woods Fisher*

God alone is the source
of all true serenity.

Ellyn Sanna

## Strength and Courage in Hope

Each and every day, just like today, I arise in the
morning afraid of what the day may bring. But then
I remember You, and I come to You in prayer. Your
Word brings me light. Your presence brings me
comfort. I breathe in Your strength and exhale my
fears. Strength in. . .fears out. I have courage of spirit
and strength of heart for all my hope—today and
every day—is in You and You alone.

*Donna K. Maltese*

*"But blessed is the man who trusts in the Lord, whose confidence is in him."*

Jeremiah 17:7 niv

Purpose

*. . .among whom you also are
the called of Jesus Christ.*

ROMANS 1:6 NASB

# Identity Crisis

Identity can be an ever-evolving thing. Most women, at one time in their lives, have been a daughter, sister, friend, wife, and, sometimes, all of those things at the same time. When those women have children, they become Mom: cook, housekeeper, babysitter, diaper changer, and more.

Your true, personal identity, though, is none of those things. Those are simply descriptions of roles that you fill. You are the called of Jesus Christ. You have been set apart and called by Him into the family of God. You are His child. That is your true identity. There is nothing any person can do to take that away from you. There are no life circumstances that will alter that identity and no way that any amount of years will cause it to fade.

Begin to see yourself as God sees you. It will make your purpose much clearer, and your roles will take on a new meaning. You need not experience grief as one stage of life moves into the next; nor should you long for the next stage or have regret over the past. You are a child of God. Your true identity will never change.

*Nicole O'Dell*

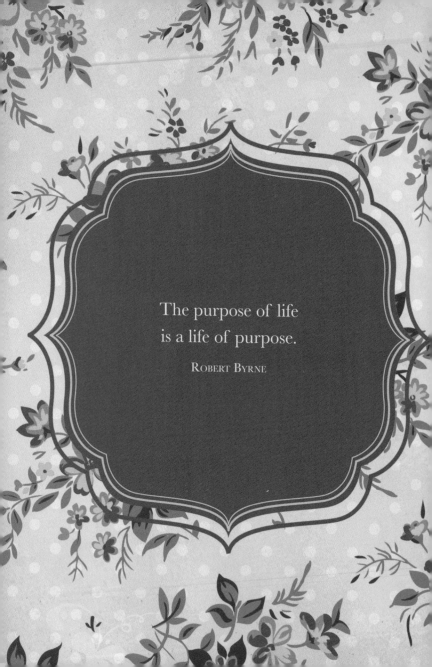

The purpose of life
is a life of purpose.

ROBERT BYRNE

## Working on Perfect

I know You're still working on me, God.
My ultimate goal is Christlikeness. I know I
won't totally achieve it while I'm on earth,
but I will do my best. With Your help, I will
come closer to the goal. I'll make mistakes,
but I won't give up. I'll keep trying until the
day I stand before You. Then I'll be like You,
for I'll see You as You are.

*Rachel Quillin*

*I will remember the deeds of the Lord;*
*yes, I will remember your miracles of long ago.*
*I will meditate on all your works and consider*
*all your mighty deeds.*

PSALM 77:11–12 NIV

# Remembering the Lord

When God created our minds, He did an amazing thing. Not only are we able to think and live in the present, but we have the ability to look back on the past. Even with today's digital photos and family videos, nothing is as complex as our memories.

As we look back on our lives, we are able to see accomplishments and maybe even a few mistakes. We may have attained certain goals. Or perhaps our plans haven't gone exactly the way we'd envisioned. Whichever the case, our bodies cannot go back to the past, but our thoughts can. Our memories open windows and opportunities for us to "change the future" because of how we deal with our past.

In the scripture above, the psalmist writes about remembering what God has done. He has done great things for us personally, but also for humankind and believers throughout the centuries. If we belong to God's family, then the miracles God performed and the works He continues to do were and are for us. Our personal stories have no DELETE button; but with God, even the worst memories can have a purpose we can turn around and use for Him.

*Kate E. Schmelzer*

We are made wise not by the
recollection of our past,
but by the responsibility for our future.

GEORGE BERNARD SHAW

# Secret Things and Revealed Things

I know there are things You don't reveal to me about my future, dear God. I'm thankful for that. I'd likely be terrified if I could see everything. But you have shown me many things so that I will better serve and obey You and teach my children to do likewise. Lord, let me please You all my days.

*Rachel Quillin*

*However, as it is written: "No eye has seen,
no ear has heard, no mind has conceived what God has
prepared for those who love him"—but God has revealed
it to us by his Spirit. The Spirit searches all things,
even the deep things of God.*

1 Corinthians 2:9–10 niv

Work

*Whatever your task, put yourselves into it,*
*as done for the Lord and not for your masters.*

COLOSSIANS 3:23 NRSV

# Renewed Mind

Claire recalled the past few years of her life—the infinite number of diapers changed, loads of laundry folded, dishes washed, floors vacuumed, meals prepared, lessons taught to her children, and thought to herself, *Isn't there more to life than this?*

The Lord tells us, "Yes!" The Lord provides a renewed mind-set for how we are to embrace these tasks as mothers. He instructs us that whatever our task (e.g., cleaning toilets, grocery shopping, teaching our children), we need to put our entire being into it as if we were polishing the pearly gates of the Almighty! We are, in fact, serving Him because everything we have—the house, the car, the children, and the bank account—belongs to God. When we have the privilege of changing diapers, washing laundry, and cooking meals, we are engaging in the very tasks the Lord has specifically called us to do for this season of our lives. We can choose to complete His work with an attitude of drudgery and boredom or reframe the task as an act of service to the Lord, giving back to the One who has blessed us with a place to live and children who call us "Mother."

*Tina Elacqua*

The ordinary acts we practice
every day at home are of more
importance to the soul than their
simplicity might suggest.

THOMAS MOORE

# Before I Was Formed

I never cease to be amazed, Lord, that even
before I was conceived, You knew the work You
had for me to do. I'm just now learning what
these responsibilities are. I've discovered that
one of my roles is to be a good mother. You
already know the plan You have for my children,
as well, and part of Your design for me is to help
mold them into people who will carry out Your
design for them.

*Rachel Quillin*

*Don't you see that children are God's best gift?*
*the fruit of the womb his generous legacy?*

<small>PSALM 127:3 MSG</small>

# The Best Investment

When viewed in terms of dollars and cents, children do not represent a great financial return. Even before birth, parents deal with the high cost of prenatal care. They buy insurance, set up payment schedules for labor and delivery charges, and purchase cribs, car seats, and strollers. When little "Her Majesty" or "His Highness" arrives, no owner's manual is included. However, an endless list of required items soon appears, including onesies, formula, and diapers by the ton. As children grow, the cost in dollars, time, and energy escalates, leaving parents with only a cluttered house and yard to show for a huge investment, and their child, of course, who continues to eat them out of house and home.

Yet God considers children one of His most precious gifts. Lovely homes with clean carpets will not last. The status of new cars and big bank accounts shrinks in comparison to hugs from chubby little arms and warm, messy kisses that melt the heart. Even more, material possessions lose their significance when we realize the muddy little people who stain the new sofa not only will make a unique impact in human history, but will live eternally. In a child, God creates a being who can reflect His image forever.

And He lets us imperfect moms help.

*Rachael Phillips*

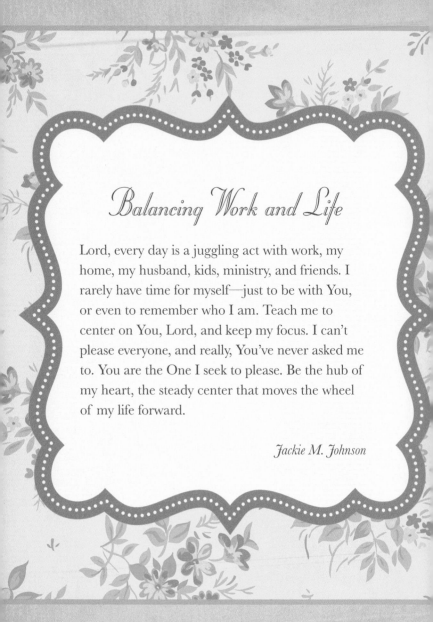

# Balancing Work and Life

Lord, every day is a juggling act with work, my home, my husband, kids, ministry, and friends. I rarely have time for myself—just to be with You, or even to remember who I am. Teach me to center on You, Lord, and keep my focus. I can't please everyone, and really, You've never asked me to. You are the One I seek to please. Be the hub of my heart, the steady center that moves the wheel of my life forward.

*Jackie M. Johnson*